PAW PRINTS IN THE BUTTER

a clowder of cats curious and comical

Patricia Feinberg Stoner

with illustrations by Judith Gordon

Dedicated with all my love to

PATRICK

without whom

and to

PURDEY

whose best friend was a cat

CONTENTS

THE OLD CURIOSITY CAT

Are there paw-prints in the butter
And a nose mark on the pane?
Is there fluff beneath the sofa?
THAT CAT's been here again!

The Old Curiosity Cat is a card:
He has to know everything, won't be debarred
From bedroom or kitchen or garage or loo.
If you're going somewhere he has to go too.

The Old Curiosity Cat is the kind
That never says "Pardon," or "Hope you don't mind."
If at midnight you creep like a mouse down the stair
The Old Curiosity Cat will be there.

If the postman has called and he's left on the mat
A brown-paper package, intriguingly fat,
Be sure that its contents won't long be in doubt:
The Old Curiosity Cat will find out!

If some new people move into Number Thirteen
He knows them already: he's already been
Inspecting their cupboards and nosing their chairs -
The Old Curiosity Cat's everywhere.

Curiosity (says the old adage) has killed
Many cats, so I tell him. He's very strong willed.
He knows with his ancient cat wisdom the fact
That *finding things out* very soon brought them
back.

There are paw-prints in the butter,
There's a nose mark on the pane,
There is fluff beneath the sofa -
THAT CAT's been here again.

NIPPENGRIPP

I know an exceedingly curious cat,
A lecherous, treacherous, furious cat
A devious, thievious, mischievious cat,
A cat who is NOT WHAT HE SEEMS.

At first you might think he's a lovable cat,
A cuddlesome, muddlesome, huggable cat,
The purriest, furriest, curliest cat,
But no: he is NOT WHAT HE SEEMS.

He'll climb on your knee for the friendliest chat,
The veriest, merriest, tenderest chat,
Amorous, clamorous, stammerous chat,
Beware - he is NOT WHAT HE SEEMS.

His teeth are the sharpest you'll see on a cat,
The keenest, the meanest to be on a cat.
He'll nip you, he'll rip you, he'll strike just like *that*!
The cat who is NOT WHAT HE SEEMS.

A means I'm devising for wising that cat,
Astounding, confounding, surprising that cat.
I'll pounce on him, bounce him, he won't go for that,
The cat who is NOT WHAT HE SEEMS.

It doesn't seem right to go hurtin' that cat,
But this is one way to make certain that cat
(The blackguard) is staggered when he finds out that

*We humans are not necessarily the soft-headed,
silly sentimentalists that to all feline kind we must
inevitably seem.*

LULU THE TERRIBLE

Lulu the Siamese kitten
Was chocolate and *café-au-lait*.
Her noble descent could be seen at a glance
In the haughty blue stare and the cheekbones aslant
And the crook at the end of her tail.

Lulu at peace could be charming
Affectionate, playful and douce.
But when crossed she was fury incarnate, a fact
Which deterred any dog with a mind to attack
This Jekyll and Hyde of a puss.

One day into town came a stranger
A bouncy, big, lolloping hound
Who (in playfulness rather than malice, no doubt)
Advanced upon Lulu, but Lulu stayed put
Disdainfully holding her ground.

For Lulu was born under Leo
And, leonine in her defence,
She sprang at his nose with her needle-sharp claws
And, spitting obscenities, made the dog pause
In the midst of his ill-judged advance.

The battle was fierce, but it lasted
No more than a moment or two.
The dog was all bluster, its menace a blind –
No match for this blazing-eyed, tail-lashing fiend
With the fury of Hell in her mew.

And after the dust had abated,
Not even remotely perturbed,
Taking victory calmly for granted, she set
To the business of finishing off the toilette
Which the foolhardy dog had disturbed.

So now when the talk turns to heroes
And feats of inspired derring-do,
Whenever the roster of heroes is told,
One name leads the rest in the ranks of the bold
The name of the mighty LULU.

LULU AND THE
TRAVELLING SALESMAN

You've heard me speak of Lulu, she's
The pugilistic Siamese
Whose pretty looks belie her fierce ambition.

Now Lulu was fastidious:
The vulgar and the hideous
She treated with a consummate derision.

And, mindful of her rank and race
She kept her passions in their place
And never stooped to common promiscuity.

She chose to mate with T'ang because
His pedigree matched hers (there was
Of eligible males no superfluity).

She kept this custom till the day
She let herself be led astray –
Or so we must suppose, for dissipation

Was not in Lulu's nature. She
Departed from fidelity
And, naturally, paid for indiscretion.

At first no-one suspected it.
You couldn't have detected it –
She seemed her usual calm and haughty self.
But, looking back, we should have guessed
The secret when she made her nest
Not on her usual bedroom cupboard shelf.

But well away from prying stares
Ensconced behind the bath, from where
She glared. And no amount of our enticing

Could budge her from her hiding place:
She skulked, as though in deep disgrace
Which, come to think of it, was not surprising.

Eventually, of course, we found
The reason why she went to ground –
That sort of thing can't very well be hidden.

The awful truth we understood
When Lulu came out with her brood:
One Siamese... and seven tabby kittens.

THE CAT WHO HAS BEEN HERE BEFORE

(The kitten sat at his feet, wide-eyed).

The Cat Who Has Been Here Before
licked a condescending paw
and began:

"You want to know about this nine lives lark?
Pin back your ears, my old son.
You've come to the right place, I can tell you.
I can tell you:
I was there.

"I knew Julius Caesar -
funny old geezer:
no time for cats at all.
Brilliant at conquering Gaul.

"I knew Dick Whittington
before he came to London.
I was the cat that looked at a king
back in fifteen hundred.

"I knew..."

*(The kitten yawned and stretched,
curled itself into a ball)*

"... Will Shakespeare, of course. His
plays weren't *all* about kings and horses.
Who was 'the cat i'the adage'? I can tell you.
I can tell you:
I was there.

"Now did I think to mention
My voyages of exploration?
I knew that foreign chappie well. What was his
name -
Columpuss?

"Am I getting your attention?

"And speaking of sailing
(*are* you attending?)
there was that business of the pea-green boat
which Edward Lear discussed with me
before he put it out to sea.

"I knew Tommy Eliot
(Possum was my cousin)
and walked and talked with Gallico
a dozen times or more.

"Oh yes, I've known them all, old son,
I've seen them come and go.
But we're the older race - you mark my words -
and we'll outlive 'em, I can tell you.
I can tell you:
I'll be there."

(The kitten, though, was fast asleep).

A PUSS IN BOOTS

In the high street chemist yesterday
Upon a thoughtfully-provided chair
Beside a radiator sat
A large and well-contented cat.
The chance was far too good to miss
For one who loves a play on words
So: "Look! A Puss in Boots!" I cried.

The shopping zombies clearly thought me mad.
They turned, as only English people turn,
A blank and even hostile stare
Upon me, standing foolish there
As "Look! A Puss in Boots!" I cried.

But then the creature stretched and purred
And opened amber eyes (that matched its fur).
And then it turned and winked at me.
I'll swear I saw it wink at me.
As "Look! A Puss in Boots!" I cried.

(*Previously published in the National Poetry Anthology 2003*)

THE CLERICAL CAT

The clerical cat, oh, the clerical cat,
  Odour of sanctity, odour of mice,
Is perfectly pious and frightfully fat,
The clerical cat that I know.

His name's Asmodeus and you might think that
A curious name for a sanctifi-cat.
But meek though he seems, yet to mouse and to rat
The Devil Incarnate, the clerical cat.

He dwells in a church along Rochester Row
Black in his colour and black in his heart.
He prowls through the vestry, he prowls as of right,
The clerical cat that I know.

And whether it's Vespers or whether it's Nones
The clerical cat wouldn't miss.
He makes the amens in the purr-fectest tones,
The clerical cat that I know.

But oh, what a hypocrite, clerical cat:
He shuns the trespass of the sinner.
His piety's worth he knows well, fatted cat -
A nice piece of fish to his dinner.

And oh, what a hypocrite, clerical cat:
He knows the rewards of the saint -
A comfortable snooze on a clerical lap
The clerical cat that I know.

The clerical cat, oh, the clerical cat,
Odour of sanctity, odour of mice,
Is perfectly pious and frightfully fat,
The clerical cat that I know.

LINES TO A THREE-NAMED CAT

Tsarina Anastasia Pickle.
Now there's a mouthful if you like.
What kind of name, you ask, is that
To dub an unsuspecting cat?

Tsarina Anastasia Pickle
Acquired her triple-pronged cognomen
Through some dissent about her lineage:

True Russian Blue she's held to be
By those that vaunt her pedigree
(which seems a bit suspect to me).
Tsarina, hence, for royalty.

Tsarina Anastasia Pickle.
As I've said, I have my doubts
About her authenticity.

So: Anastasia. Wrong or right
I gravely fear that patch of white
Upon her bosom means she might
Not be quite... quite.

Tsarina Anastasia Pickle.
Pickle? What a name! Poor Puss
to be encumbered thus.

I'll tell you why - and it's a sin:
She'd been abandoned - in a bin!
Unkempt, unwanted, starveling thin
A right old pickle to be in.

Tsarina Anastasia Pickle.
She likes it, so do I.
For all it is a mouthful, we're
Content, my three-named cat and I.
☐

THE STATIONERY CAT

Sing a song of paperclips
Inky paws and whiskertips.
Here's a novel kind of puss:
The stationery cat.

The preferred habitat
Of the stationery cat
Is the writer's proverbial hovel.
He'll dabble his toes
In your Proustian prose
And upset the ink on your novel.

But don't infer that
The stationery cat
Is gifted with lit'ry pretensions.
'Tis not the Pulitzer
He craves, not a whit, sir:
His ambition has lesser dimensions.

If the truth be revealed
It's the pen that you wield
That engrosses this pussycat wholly.
He'd rather have blotters
Than catnip or bloaters,
He'd rather have carbon than coley.

He's not over-keen
One the Word Processing scene
And the whole electronic caboodle.
Since he was a kitten
He's loved things hand-written
And the thoughtful abstract of the doodle

He's exceptionally fond
Of white A4 bond
Which he'll nest in with joyous abandon.
The desktop is ace
For a catnapping place
And a keyboard is perfect to stand on.

Though "Puss off!" I say
He won't go away,
And that is the reason I'm griping.
For -)(!"£$^&*_)(&*$!**!\?... (oh, drat!
That stationery cat
Has just tried his paw at some typing).

Whatever I do
He simply won't shoo
I can't get him out of the picture.
With his tail in the ink
And his nose in my drink
That stationery cat is a fixture.

But when I complete
A work to compete
With *Candide* or *Anna Karenina,*
As I grow rich and fat
'Twill be thanks to the cat
For keeping me hard at my pen in 'ere.

So smile and sing of paperclips
Inky paws and whiskertips.
Here's my favourite kind of puss
The stationery cat!

THE BALLADE OF
OTTOLINE AND CABRIOLE
(or: *Amor Vincit Omnia*)

Come all ye who claim that affairs of the heart
And delicate feeling set humans apart.

Come hark to my tale, if you listen you'll learn
How creatures domestic with passion can burn.

I'll sing you the saga of fair Ottoline
An elegant beauty, a calico queen.

I'll sing of her suitor, who Cabriole hight,
An ancient arthritic, a piteous sight;

His legs like parentheses, bandy and lame,
One ear was in tatters, his tail was the same -

The outcome it seems of a scrap with a dog.
To make matters worse, this unsavoury mog

Had stripes which hung drooping from whisker to
paw
Like the uniform worn by a felon of yore.

Now it chanced that one day when the spring was in
bloom,
Fair Ottoline paced up and down in her room.

Beset by those hungers which come to us all
She voiced her desires in a shrill cat-erwaul.

The toms of the neighbourhood answered in kind
And flocked to her side with but one thing in mind.

Aloof from the throng, Cabriole stood alone
And sang his amours in a crack'd baritone.

To choose from so many the lady declined.
She fled, they pursued. Cabriole came behind

Refusing, though limping, to give up the chase
He followed, determined to stay in the race.

They raced through the house then they dashed up
the stair
And on to the balcony, cornered her there.

She leapt with a negligent grace to the rail
And sat there flirtatiously grooming her tail.

Below raged the battle, and how the fur flew
As tabby faced ginger with ear-splitting mew.

They tumbled and growled as they fought for the
prize.
Now Cabriole, wicked old roué, was wise:

He bided his time and awaited his chance
Till he judged the time right for strategic advance.

Then he joined the affray with a spine-chilling yell,
Came down on those cats like a fiend out of hell.

They hadn't a hope: it was over and done
Before you could say 'Puss in boots!' He had won.

To the victor the spoils. Cabriole wasn't shy:
He claimed his reward, which she didn't deny.

And not too long afterwards, to his amaze
She made him a Dad - of five Cabriolets!
□

DIES IRAE

I am the cat who howls in the night.
I am the banshee wail
That starts you from your sleep in fright
That sets your short neck-hairs upright
That tells you all is far from right.
I am the cat who prowls in the night.

I am the cat who prowls in the night.
I am the godless shriek
That chills your curdled blood with dread
That terrifies you in your bed
That echoes in your quaking head.
I am the cat who yowls in the night.

I am the cat who yowls in the night.
I am the screech of doom
That sets you quaking in the dark
Afraid to sleep, afraid to hark
Praying for a friendly bark.
I am the cat who howls in the night.

(previously published in 'Through the Eyes of a Poet')

Patricia Feinberg Stoner began her career as a graduate trainee with the Liverpool Daily Post. Quickly discovering she was a terrible reporter, she switched to feature writing and since then her career has revolved around the written word, as a journalist, advertising copywriter and publicist.

For many years she was international press officer for Granada Television, leaving to set up her own publicity business, The Good Word.

Now retired, she devotes her time to writing short stories and poetry (mainly humorous verse) which have been published in various print and online anthologies. She is a member of Scribes, a U3A creative writing group.

Patricia lives in West Sussex with her husband Patrick, also a writer, and a lunatic Brittany spaniel who loves cats. You can contact her via Facebook (Patricia Stoner).

Proceeds from 'Paw Prints in the Butter' are donated to WADARS, a local animal rescue and rehoming charity.

Printed in Great Britain
by Amazon.co.uk, Ltd.,
Marston Gate.